Title V   2005

Innovative Programs Grant

MATHWORKS!

Using Math to

Solve a CRIME

by
Wendy and David Clemson,
Kev Pritchard, and Dr. Allison Jones

GARETH STEVENS
GS
PUBLISHING
A World Almanac Education Group Company

POLICE LINE - DO NOT CROSS

Please visit our web site at: www.garethstevens.com
For a free color catalog describing Gareth Stevens Publishing's
list of high-quality books and multimedia programs, call
1-800-542-2595 (USA) or 1-800-387-3178 (Canada).
Gareth Stevens Publishing's fax: (414) 332-3567.

Library of Congress Cataloging-in-Publication Data

Clemson, Wendy.
    Using math to solve a crime / by Wendy Clemson . . .
[et al.]. — North American ed.
        p. cm. — (Mathworks!)
    ISBN 0-8368-4213-8 (lib. bdg.)
    1. Mathematics—Problems, exercises, etc.—Juvenile
literature. 2. Criminal investigation—Juvenile literature.
I. Clemson, Wendy. II. Series.
    QA43.U855   2004
    510'.76—dc22   2004047841

This North American edition first published in 2005 by
Gareth Stevens Publishing
A World Almanac Education Group Company
330 West Olive Street, Suite 100
Milwaukee, Wisconsin 53212

This U.S. edition copyright © 2005 by Gareth Stevens Inc.
Original edition copyright © 2004 by ticktock Entertainment
Ltd. First published in Great Britain in 2004 by ticktock Media
Ltd., Unit 2, Orchard Business Centre, North Farm Road,
Tunbridge Wells, Kent, TN2 3XF, England.

The publishers thank the following consultants for their
kind assistance: Jenni Back and Liz Pumfrey (NRICH Project,
Cambridge University) and Debra Voege (Science and Math
Curriculum Resource Teacher), with special thanks to
Lorna Cowan.

Gareth Stevens Editor: Dorothy L. Gibbs
Gareth Stevens Art Direction: Tammy West

Photo credits (t=top, b=bottom, c=center, l=left, r=right)
Alamy: cover, 1, 6, 8-9(c), 12, 13, 16(br), 19(t),
21(background), 22.

Printed in the United States of America

1 2 3 4 5 6 7 8 9 08 07 06 05 04

CONTENTS

HAVE FUN WITH MATH

How to Use This Book

Math is important in the daily lives of people everywhere. We use math when we play games, ride bicycles, or go shopping, and everyone uses math at work. Imagine there has been a burglary at the home of a millionaire. You may not realize it, but police officers, detectives, and forensic scientists would use math to find evidence to solve a crime. In this book, you will be able to try lots of exciting math activities as you learn what it is like to be part of a crime-solving team. If you can work with numbers, measurements, shapes, charts, and diagrams, then you could **SOLVE A CRIME**.

How does it feel to be a detective?

Grab your evidence kit and find out what it is like to investigate the scene of a crime.

Math Activities

The detective's clipboards have math activities for you to try. Get your pencil, ruler, and notebook (for figuring out problems and listing answers).

WITNESS STATEMENTS

You have several good pieces of evidence from the mansion crime scene — footprints, broken glass splashed with blood, a hair, a palm print, and some fingerprints. More than just physical evidence such as fingerprints, however, is gathered at a crime scene. Detectives also gather verbal, or spoken, evidence by taking statements from witnesses, victims, and suspects. One of the millionaire's neighbors has given you some interesting information. The neighbor is an elderly woman who cannot walk very well, so she spends her days looking out the window. Earlier today, she saw someone, dressed in black and wearing a hat, running from the mansion's back gate.

Detective Work

The person the millionaire's neighbor saw was also wearing white athletic shoes and glasses. The neighbor is not sure of the person's height, but he or she was definitely taller than the garden wall, which is 66 inches high.

You have interviewed everyone who lives or works at the mansion, or who was seen in the vicinity on the day of the burglary, and you have listed their answers to your questions in the DATA BOX on page 15. You asked each person's height and if he or she ever wears glasses or owns a pair of white athletic shoes.

Use the information in the DATA BOX to answer the following questions:

1) How many people never wear glasses?
2) Who does not own white athletic shoes?
3) Which two suspects are the same height?
4) What is the difference in height between the tallest suspect and the shortest suspect?
5) Which of the suspects could the millionaire's neighbor have seen leaving the grounds?

  (Be sure to write the names of the suspects in your own notebook.)

14

Police Work Fact

When an evidence technician interviews the victim of a crime, or any witnesses, he or she asks questions that help the people being interviewed describe the suspect. Then the evidence technician uses special computer software to produce a likeness of the offender's face.

NEED HELP?

• If you are not sure how to do some of the math problems, turn to pages 28 and 29, where you will find lots of tips to help get you started.

• Turn to pages 30 and 31 to check your answers.
(Try all the activities and challenges before you look at the answers.)

• Turn to page 32 for definitions of some words and terms used in this book.

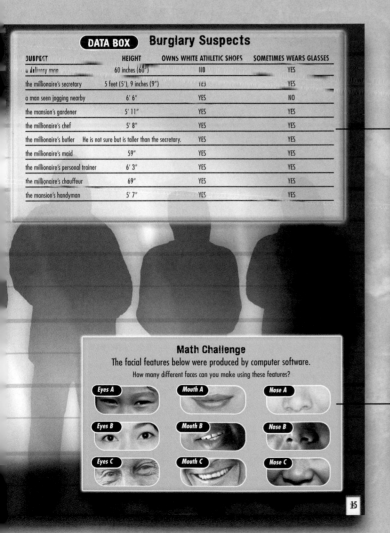

DATA BOX — Burglary Suspects			
SUSPECT	HEIGHT	OWNS WHITE ATHLETIC SHOES	SOMETIMES WEARS GLASSES
a delivery man	60 inches (60")	NO	YES
the millionaire's secretary	5 feet (5'), 9 inches (9")	YES	YES
a man seen jogging nearby	6' 6"	YES	NO
the mansion's gardener	5' 11"	YES	YES
the millionaire's chef	5' 8"	YES	YES
the millionaire's butler	He is not sure but is taller than the secretary.	YES	YES
the millionaire's maid	59"	YES	YES
the millionaire's personal trainer	6' 3"	YES	YES
the millionaire's chauffeur	69"	YES	YES
the mansion's handyman	5' 7"	YES	YES

Math Challenge
The facial features below were produced by computer software.
How many different faces can you make using these features?

Eyes A Mouth A Nose A
Eyes B Mouth B Nose B
Eyes C Mouth C Nose C

15

Math Facts and Data

To complete some of the math activities, you will need information from a DATA BOX, which looks like this. Some information will be on maps or pictures. A detective needs to examine all possibilities.

Math Challenge

Blue boxes, like this one, have extra math questions to challenge you. Give them a try!

You will find lots of amazing details about detective work, crime scenes, and forensic scientists in FACT boxes that look like this.

There has been a burglary at the mansion of a local millionaire. The millionaire is away on his yacht. His maid discovered the crime and called 911. The first police officer to arrive at the scene of a crime uses police tape to secure the scene. The police tape stops people from walking onto the scene and destroying evidence. Next, the officer, who is often called the first responding officer, calls for any assistance needed, such as a detective, an evidence technician, and, if anyone is injured, an ambulance. You are the detective on duty today. Grab your notebook and pencil — it's time to get to work!

DETECTIVE WORK

The safe is empty! All the thief left behind are some paper bands that had been wrapped around bundles of cash and some empty boxes in which the millionaire kept his jewels.

In the DATA BOX on page 7, you will see the bands that came off the missing money.

1) How much cash was stolen?

Look at the three jewel boxes in the DATA BOX. The missing gems have left the following five shapes in the boxes:
- equilateral triangle • square • octagon
- isosceles triangle • hexagon

2) Name the box in which each shape appears.

The value of each gem is as follows:
- diamond $1,000 • sapphire $850 • ruby $650

3) What is the total value of all stolen
   a) sapphires?
   b) rubies?
   c) diamonds?

Police Work Fact

The first police officer to arrive at the scene of a crime starts the investigation. The officer's work attempts to answer the following questions: What has happened? What evidence has been left behind? Does any evidence need protection from the weather? Where is the perpetrator now?

Crime Scene Fact

Depending on the type of crime, different specialists will be called to assist at a crime scene. These specialists can include evidence technicians; forensic scientists; police dog handlers and their dogs, when searching for drugs or explosives; and fire officials, for arson investigations.

What Was Stolen?

Box A: sapphires   **Box B: rubies**   **Box C: diamonds**

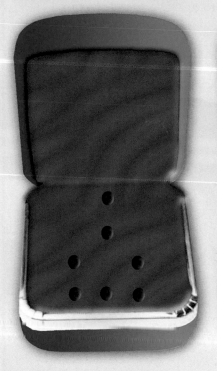

$1,000 $1,000 $1,000 $500

$500 $500 $500 $500

Math Challenge

The thief dropped the code numbers he or she used to figure out the combination for the safe.

The combination is made up of products from the 12 times (multiplication) table. Can you figure out the combination?

17	29	24	13	12
8	36	72	58	97
6	48	11	5	54	26

THE CRIME SCENE

The burglary took place in the dining room of the mansion, where a safe is hidden behind a family portrait. The dining room is now a crime scene and will be examined by an expert evidence technician. The evidence technician is in charge of the crime scene and is responsible for protecting the area and everything in it. He or she has the power to stop other people, even other police officers, from entering the scene. Evidence technicians must pay attention to every detail, no matter how small. They cannot make mistakes! Examining the crime scene is the most important part of a criminal investigation. Missing a piece of evidence could ruin a case.

Evidence Work

When an evidence technician examines a crime scene, he or she takes photographs of the scene from all angles. The evidence technician also sketches the crime scene to show the positions of doors and windows and the distances between all objects in the area.

Study the photograph to the right, which shows the dining room in the millionaire's mansion after the burglary. Try to keep a picture of the crime scene in your head.

On page 9, you will see four different sketches of the dining room.

1) Which sketch is a correct "picture" of the dining room?
2) How can you tell?

Police Work Facts

- An evidence technician checks the the police tape at a crime scene and adjusts the size of the scene if he or she thinks the area should be bigger or smaller.

- The photographs taken by an evidence technician on a crime scene are used to support prosecution of the crime in court. Both the photographs and the evidence technician's sketches can be used at a later date to check any details about the crime scene.

- An evidence technician thoroughly searches the crime scene for evidence. To keep track of the evidence, each item is assigned a unique number in a system of consecutive numbers.

Crime Scene Fact

Everyone entering a crime scene must wear protective clothing to keep hairs and clothing fibers from contaminating the scene. While working at a crime scene, an evidence technician wears a one-piece paper suit with a hood, as well as a face mask, gloves, and overshoes.

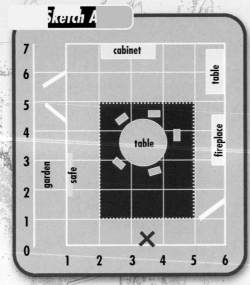

Sketch A

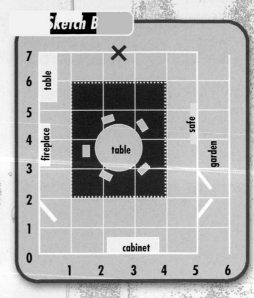

Sketch B

The red "x" on each sketch shows where you are standing. Your position will help you match the sketch to the photograph.

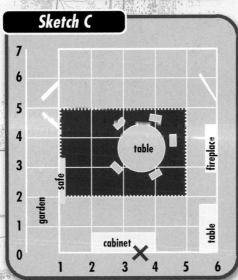

Sketch C

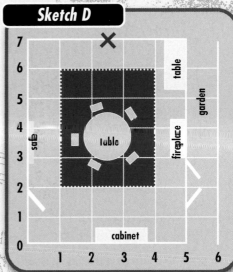

Sketch D

Math Challenge

In his or her crime scene report, the evidence technician lists all the items recovered (found) at the scene. After you have figured out which of the sketches above is the correct sketch of the room, you can use the grid on the sketch to find some clues.

The following pieces of evidence and their grid references are listed
in the evidence technician's crime scene report:

- muddy footprints (5,2)   • splashes of blood on broken glass (6,2)
- fingerprints (3,4) (0,4) (5,5)   • a palm print (2,4)   • a single hair (5,4)

1) Which clue or clues were found a) outside the French doors?   b) behind the picture in the safe?
c) just inside the French doors?   2) Where were fingerprints found?   3) Where was a palm print found?

9

EXAMINING THE SCENE

When searching a crime scene, two very important areas to examine are the point of entry, or "ingress," and the point of exit, or "egress." At the mansion, you examine the French doors in the dining room. It looks as if the perpetrator used the French doors to enter and exit the building. There are footprints in the dining room, just inside the French doors, and you find fragments of glass just outside the doors and notice that one of the window panes on the French doors has been broken. You also notice splashes of blood on the glass. The thief must have been cut when he or she smashed the glass to break in!

Detective Work

The perpetrator must have escaped through the mansion's garden, so the police are searching the grounds. Figure out how long it would take someone to run from one location to another on the grounds of the mansion.

1) If a person runs 200 yards (yds.) in one minute, how long will it take that person to run

   a) from the main gate to the mansion?
   b) from the main gate to the garage and stables?
   c) from the summerhouse to the lake, by way of the greenhouse?

2) If the distance from the back gate to the boathouse turn is 300 yards, how long does it take to run from the boathouse to the mansion?

3) How much longer does it take to run from the tennis court to the summerhouse, than from the tennis court to the mansion?

THE MILLIONAIRE'S ESTATE

PIER

MAIN GATE

GATEHOUSE

Crime Scene Fact

If a crime scene is inside a building, the evidence technician begins searching at the point of entry onto the property, such as through the garden, and moves toward the main focus of the crime, such as a safe, then to the point of exit from the property.

Math Challenge

This diagram shows some of the buildings and features on the mansion grounds.

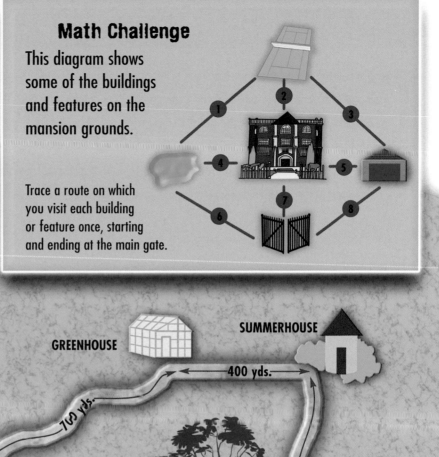

Trace a route on which you visit each building or feature once, starting and ending at the main gate.

BACK GATE

LAKE

GREENHOUSE

SUMMERHOUSE

400 yds.

700 yds.

BOATHOUSE

300 yds.

1,000 yds.

900 yds.

POOL

1,000 yds.

DRIVEWAY

MANSION

600 yds.

TENNIS COURT

500 yds.

900 yds.

GARAGE

STABLES

GATHERING EVIDENCE

The crime scene at the mansion has been photographed and sketched. Now the evidence technician must find and gather forensic evidence from the scene. Any piece of evidence that is found has to be securely packaged, then labeled with the details of where it was found, when, and by whom. The most common types of evidence found at crime scenes are blood, hairs, fiber from clothing, fragments of glass, tiny chips or slivers of paint, soil and plant material, fingerprints, footwear prints, articles of clothing, and documents. When all the forensic evidence is recovered, the evidence technician examines the scene for fingerprints.

Evidence Work

You have already shown that you can examine a crime scene. Now, it's time to find out how good you are at looking for details.

Compare the two photographs of the dining room on page 13.
1) How many differences you can find?
2) What are they?

An evidence technician recovers droplets of blood from a piece of broken glass.

Math Challenge

Fingerprints are usually "latent," which means they cannot be seen in normal light. Evidence technicians use many different techniques to find fingerprints and make them visible. Then the fingerprints can be photographed, or lifted with clear tape.

Estimate the number of fingerprints that appear on pages 12 and 13. Write down your estimate in your notebook, then actually count the fingerprints to see how good you are at estimating.

Police Work Fact

Fingerprints found at a crime scene must be compared to control samples, or elimination prints, from people who actually live or work at the scene. Elimination prints are either found at the crime scene or are taken at a later date. Comparing fingerprints to control samples helps determine whether the prints at the crime scene belong to a perpetrator or to one of the residents.

Crime Scene Fact

Each piece of evidence is photographed before being recovered. Tool marks and footwear prints are usually photographed next to a rulerlike scale. Back at the lab, the photographs are enlarged to life size.

Dining Room A

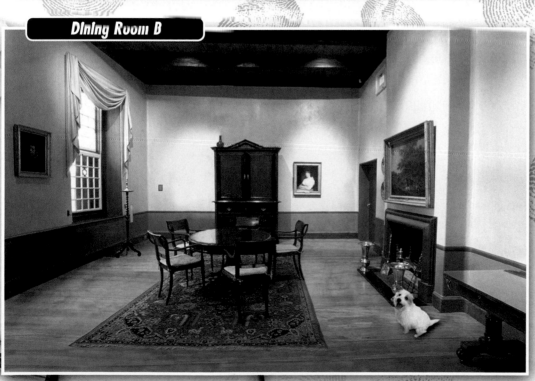

Dining Room B

Handling Evidence

BLOOD

Pools of blood are recovered using a pipette. Blood that has soaked into material is allowed to dry. Then, the material is packaged in a plastic bag or container. Dried blood is removed using a razor blade or a cotton swab dampened with water.

HAIRS

Normally, hairs are large enough to see. Evidence technicians use tweezers to pick them up, or they lift the hairs, using a special kind of tape.

FINGERPRINTS

Evidence technicians find fingerprints by shining special lights on them, by brushing them with special powders, or by applying chemicals that turn them to a color that can be seen. All of these methods help make the prints show up against their backgrounds. Sometimes, large objects believed to have prints on them are removed from the scene and taken to a lab for enhancement.

GLASS

Pieces of broken glass are put into plastic containers or boxes. Evidence glass is not put into plastic bags, because the broken glass could cut through, and it is not put into glass containers, because they could break and mix in with the evidence glass.

You have several good pieces of evidence from the mansion crime scene — footprints, broken glass splashed with blood, a hair, a palm print, and some fingerprints. More than just physical evidence such as fingerprints, however, is gathered at a crime scene. Detectives also gather verbal, or spoken, evidence by taking statements from witnesses, victims, and suspects. One of the millionaire's neighbors has given you some interesting information. The neighbor is an elderly woman who cannot walk very well, so she spends her days looking out the window. Earlier today, she saw someone, dressed in black and wearing a hat, running from the mansion's back gate.

Detective Work

The person the millionaire's neighbor saw was also wearing white athletic shoes and glasses. The neighbor is not sure of the person's height, but he or she was definitely taller than the garden wall, which is 66 inches high.

You have interviewed everyone who lives or works at the mansion, or who was seen in the vicinity on the day of the burglary, and you have listed their answers to your questions in the DATA BOX on page 15. You asked each person's height and if he or she ever wears glasses or owns a pair of white athletic shoes.

Use the information in the DATA BOX to answer the following questions:

1) How many people never wear glasses?
2) Who does not own white athletic shoes?
3) Which two suspects are the same height?
4) What is the difference in height between the tallest suspect and the shortest suspect?
5) Which of the suspects could the millionaire's neighbor have seen leaving the grounds?

(Be sure to write the names of the suspects in your own notebook.)

Police Work Fact

When an evidence technician interviews the victim of a crime, or any witnesses, he or she asks questions that help the people being interviewed describe the suspect. Then the evidence technician uses special computer software to produce a likeness of the offender's face.

DATA BOX Burglary Suspects

SUSPECT	HEIGHT	OWNS WHITE ATHLETIC SHOES	SOMETIMES WEARS GLASSES
a delivery man	60 inches (60")	NO	YES
the millionaire's secretary	5 feet (5'), 9 inches (9")	YES	YES
a man seen jogging nearby	6' 6"	YES	NO
the mansion's gardener	5' 11"	YES	YES
the millionaire's chef	5' 8"	YES	YES
the millionaire's butler	He is not sure but is taller than the secretary.	YES	YES
the millionaire's maid	59"	YES	YES
the millionaire's personal trainer	6' 3"	YES	YES
the millionaire's chauffeur	69"	YES	YES
the mansion's handyman	5' 7"	YES	YES

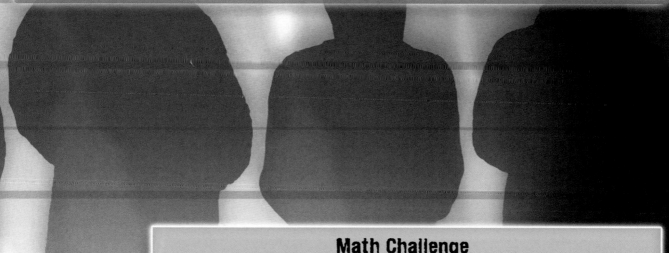

Math Challenge

The facial features below were produced by computer software.
How many different faces can you make using these features?

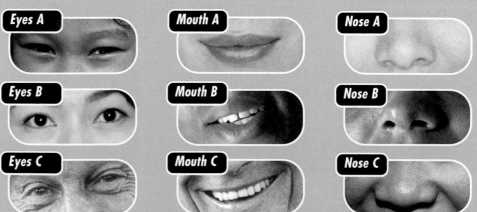

Eyes A

Eyes B

Eyes C

Mouth A

Mouth B

Mouth C

Nose A

Nose B

Nose C

INTERVIEWING SUSPECTS

You have narrowed down the suspects to seven people who could have been the mysterious figure the millionaire's neighbor saw running from the grounds of the mansion. Do you have the correct seven people written down in your notes? The maid has said that she discovered the crime. She told you that when she finished dusting in the dining room, at 3:40 p.m., all was well. When she returned with a vase of fresh flowers for the table, at 4:00 p.m., the French doors were wide open, and the safe was empty! You now have to find out what all of the suspects were doing at the time the crime was committed.

Detective Work

Pages 16 and 17 contain statements from all seven suspects. Each suspect was asked what he or she was doing on the day of the burglary from 2:00 p.m. onward.

Read the statements and figure out which suspects could have been at the mansion between 3:40 p.m. and 4:00 p.m. and had enough time to commit the crime.

(Remember to write down the names of the suspects in your notebook.)

SUSPECT STATEMENT
Personal Trainer

The personal trainer says he was alone in the summerhouse, doing yoga for 45 minutes, then lifting weights for about three-quarters of an hour. He started at 2:00 p.m.

SUSPECT STATEMENT
Chef

The chef started making bread at 2:00 p.m. His timetable was as follows:
- set out ingredients and make dough (10 minutes)
- make soup while dough rises (20 minutes)
- knead dough and let it rise again (5 minutes)
- put dough in oven, clean up the kitchen, and wait for bread to bake (35 minutes)

SUSPECT STATEMENT
Secretary

The secretary's watch is broken. She says she was in her office at the gatehouse, typing letters, then left the gatehouse, through the main gate, and walked to the village to mail the letters, but she does not know at what time. It takes 40 minutes to walk to the post office.

SUSPECT STATEMENT
Gardener

The gardener was busy all afternoon in the greenhouse, planting rose cuttings. He started at 2:00 p.m. and planted 12 rose cuttings. It took him 8 minutes to plant each cutting.

SUSPECT STATEMENT
Handyman

The handyman started painting railings near the gatehouse at 2:00 p.m. There are 28 railings, and each one takes 5 minutes to paint. (You observe that all the railings were painted.) The handyman says he saw the secretary leave with some letters in her hand as the church clock struck the half hour, and he saw the chauffeur drive in through the main gate soon after that.

SUSPECT STATEMENT
Butler

The butler sat down in kitchen at 2:00 p.m. to prepare next week's work schedule, which takes 11 minutes per day to write out.

SUSPECT STATEMENT
Chauffeur

The chauffeur says she started cleaning the car at 2:00 p.m. The cleaning took 55 minutes. Then she drove to the village to fill the car with gas. She thinks the trip to the village took about 35 minutes.

Math Challenge

The chauffeur has just remembered the exact time at which she returned to the mansion.

She remembers seeing the church clock in her rearview mirror as she drove through the main gate. What time does the clock show?

(Remember, the face of the clock was reversed because it was seen in a mirror.)

The pieces of evidence collected at the crime scene have been taken to a laboratory, so it is time to do some forensic work and eliminate some more suspects. Footwear prints can be as unique as fingerprints. As we walk around in our shoes each day, we wear them down, and they become damaged by stones or small pieces of glass. This damage is unique, which means that no other shoes will have the same damage pattern. A footwear print recovered from a crime scene can be compared to a suspect's shoe, proving that the shoe was or was not at the crime scene. Footwear marks will be either "latent" (cannot be seen) or "patent" (can be seen).

Forensic Work

The footprints found in the dining room at the mansion are patent. No one was allowed to come in or go out of the French doors until the footprints had been photographed and recovered.

The two footprints measured 12 inches long and 11 inches long.
1) According to the bar graph below what shoe sizes are they?

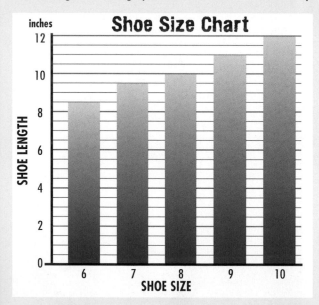

The DATA BOX on page 19 shows the shoe sizes of the remaining suspects. 2) Who could have made the footprints?

12 inches

11 inches

Casting Footprints

A print left by footwear in mud is three-dimensional. After the mud has dried, the print can be cast. The casting process involves: 1) pushing a plastic frame that looks like a small fence into the ground around the print; 2) mixing a casting compound; 3) pouring the compound into the print, inside the frame; 4) after the compound has hardened, lifting the cast out of the frame and transporting it to a laboratory to be examined.

Lab technicians match footwear to footprints.

Lifting Footprints

One way to recover footwear prints from hard surfaces is by using ESLA (electrostatic lifting apparatus). The process involves: 1) rolling a special plastic sheet over the print; 2) passing electric current through the sheet, which attracts dust particles from the print to the sheet in the shape of the print; 3) sending the plastic sheet to a lab; 4) shining a powerful light over the sheet so the prints can be seen and photographed.

Sometimes, special paper treated with adhesive or gelatin is used to lift footprints. The paper, which is like a large sticky label, is placed over the print for a few minutes. When the sticky paper is lifted, dust or mud from the footwear is transferred onto the paper in the shape of the print.

Math Challenge

Every pair of shoes has a manufactured sole pattern. Sole patterns are stored in a computer database. Forensic scientists can use information from the database to help them determine the make and model of a shoe.

Study the shoe soles below. The mud on the soles fills a fraction of each sole's pattern.
1) What are the fractions? 2) Convert the fractions for shoes b and d to decimals.

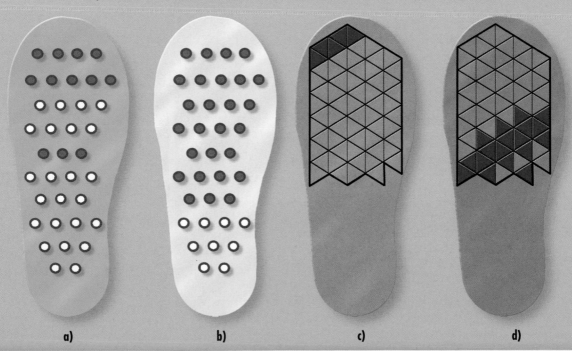

a)   b)   c)   d)

ANALYZING CLUES: BLOOD AND HAIR

Now, the blood splashes and the single hair that were found at the crime scene must be analyzed. The blood has been removed from the pieces of broken glass and is being tested to find out if it is type A, B, AB, or O. All humans have one of these four blood types. The single hair has been mounted on a microscope slide. A microscope will magnify the hair one hundred times its normal size for close examination. Forensic scientists can then tell whether it is human hair or animal hair, and they can confirm the color of the hair. By examining the tip of the hair, scientists can tell if the hair has been cut recently and whether it was cut with scissors or clippers.

Forensic Work

The blood found at the crime scene is type B, and the hair found in the safe is brown. Eliminate more suspects by comparing their hair colors and blood groups.

Drawing up a chart like the one below is a good way to compare the suspects. One suspect has been put into the chart already.

BLOOD TYPE	HAIR COLOR	
	brown	not brown
blood type B		
not blood type B		

Draw the chart in your notebook and put the other suspects into the correct sections. Who could still be the perpetrator?

GARDENER
brown hair / blood type B

CHEF
brown hair / blood type A

Blood Fact

For many years, doctors tried to transfer blood from one person to another, but the transfer, or transfusion, often failed. The blood would get lumpy and kill the patient. In 1901, however, a scientist named Carl Landsteiner discovered that all blood is not the same. Landsteiner found four different types of blood and determined that a blood transfusion will work only if the right type of blood is transferred.

Hair Facts

A single hair has three layers: 1) the cuticle (outer covering), 2) the cortex (inner part), and 3) the medulla (a tube through the center of the cortex). The cuticle is made of colorless scales that overlap like the shingles on a roof. The shape of the scales can be used to tell whether a hair is from a human or an animal. The cortex contains pigment granules that give hair its color.

Hair is often found at a crime scene because, every day, approximately one hundred hairs fall out of a person's head. Sometimes, eyebrows, eyelashes, facial hairs, and hairs from arms or legs are found. Under a microscope, the hairs from different areas of the human body look different.

PERSONAL TRAINER
hlack hair / blood type O

Math Challenge

About two or three weeks after a haircut, hair tips begin to look rounded. The tip of the single hair found at the crime scene looks square, which means it was probably cut recently.

You visit the village hairdresser to find out if any of the brown-haired suspects have had a haircut in the last week. The hairdresser checks a tally of her customers for the week.

HAIR COLOR	NUMBER OF CUSTOMERS
BROWN	//// //// ////
BLACK	////
WHITE	//// ///
RED	//
BLOND	//// //

Look at the hairdresser's tally fo answer the following questions:

1) How many customers did the hairdresser have?
2) How many customers did not have white hair?
3) Six customers have dyed hair. What fraction is that of the total number of customers?

BUTLER
brown hair / blood type B

ANALYZING CLUES: FINGERPRINTS

Θ he patterns of ridges on people's hands, fingers, and thumbs are unique to each person. Our ridge patterns form before we are born and stay the same our whole lives, unless they are damaged by burns or severe scarring. There are sweat pores along the lengths of the ridges, so when a finger touches a suitable surface, it leaves a thin, usually invisible, impression in sweat. The impression is called a fingerprint. A fingerprint can prove that a particular person was at a crime scene, but it cannot prove when. Police officers will compare fingerprints found at a crime scene with inked fingerprints taken from suspects, the victim, and any other people who were at the scene.

Forensic Work

When fingerprints match, identification is "absolute," which means that the person was definitely at the scene.

Look carefully at these partial finger-prints found in the safe at the millionaire's mansion. Which of the inked fingerprints do they match?

5)

4)

3)

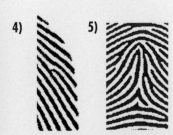

INKED FINGERPRINTS

millionaire

butler

gardener

Police officers use ink to get samples of fingerprints from crime suspects.

22

Main Classes of Fingerprints

PLAIN ARCH   **TENTED ARCH**

ARCHES

The ridges enter from one side and exit at the other. Arch fingerprints can be subdivided into plain arches and tented arches.

SPIRAL WHORL

WHORLS

A spiral whorl contains at least one ridge that makes a complete 360° turn around the print.

PLAIN LOOP

LOOPS

Loops generally have at least one ridge that starts on one side, extends across the finger, then curves back again.

Galton's Details

Besides identifying fingerprints by class, each fingerprint has certain characteristics, known as Galton's details, that can be useful when comparing prints. Four of the five main ridge characteristics are shown below.

ending ridge

enclosure

bifurcation, or forked ridge

dot, or island

The butler's palm is 92 square centimeters.

The gardener's palm is 87 square centimeters.

Math Challenge

Count the whole squares in this palm print found on the table in the dining room. Each whole square is one square centimeter, so you can find the area of the palm print in square centimeters.

1) To whom does this palm print belong?
2) Find the area of the palm of your hand in square inches.
3) What is the the area of your palm in square centimeters?
4) What is the difference between the area of your palm and the gardener's?

CONFRONTING THE SUSPECT

The village hairdresser has just confirmed that the gardener had his hair cut last week. All of the evidence is now pointing toward just one person — the gardener! He had enough time to commit the crime. It could be his footprint in the dining room, his palm print on the table, his blood on the broken glass, and his hair in the safe. The fingerprints found in the safe were definitely the gardener's. It is time to confront your main suspect. You find the gardener in the greenhouse. He is acting suspiciously and refuses to answer any questions, so you arrest him, then take a look around.

Detective Work

Before he was arrested, the gardener was busy making a note that looks like some kind of code. Cracking codes is a specialist's skill, but the DATA BOX on page 25 has a grid that will help you decipher the gardener's secret message.

To make a letter from the grid, you need two numbers, one number for the row and one number for the column. The number 15, for example, stands for row "1" and column "5," which is the letter "e." The number 43 is the letter "r," and number 51 is either "u" or "v."

Use the grid to crack the code so you can read the gardener's note on page 25.

When an arrest is made, the suspect is usually put in handcuffs.

Evidence Fact

Every piece of evidence gathered at a crime scene must have "a chain of evidence," which is a written record that tells everything that has happened to the piece of evidence from the moment is was recovered at the crime scene until it appears in court. Every police officer or scientist who comes into contact with the evidence must keep the chain going. If there are any gaps in the chain, that piece of evidence could be considered inadmissible, which means that it could not be used in court to help convict the perpetrator of the crime.

Forensics Fact

Evidence found at a crime scene helps investigators link a suspect to the crime. If you found the gardener's athletic shoes, you could compare them to the footprint found at the scene of the crime. The footprint contains important details from the sole of a shoe. The unique damage marks on the sole of the gardener's shoe could prove that he was at the scene of the crime.

DATA BOX · Code Cracker

	1	2	3	4	5
1	a	b	c	d	e
2	f	g	h	i	j
3	k	l	m	n	o
4	p	q	r	s	t
5	u v	w	x	y	z

2235   4535   452315   45431515

4435514523   3521   452315

22431515342335514415

113414   31354345735154445

3521   452315   451534342444

1335514345   113414   32353531

2434   452315   23353215

2434   452315   4543513431

Math Challenge

Make up your own secret code by giving each letter of the alphabet a number, from 1 to 26, and start with the first letter of your name as number "1."

FINDING THE STOLEN GOODS

The evidence found at the crime scene, the analysis of the evidence by forensic scientists, and the interviews you have conducted with the witnesses and the suspects have all paid off. The main suspect, the gardener, has confessed! But you still have one small problem. The gardener hid the money and the jewels so that, in the event he was arrested, an accomplice would be able to pick them up and keep them for him. You must find the stolen goods and return them to the millionaire before you can close the case. You will also have to find out who the gardener's accomplice is — but that's another case entirely!

Detective Work

You are standing at the tree with the hole in its trunk. Inside the hole, you find a note for the gardener's accomplice. The note gives directions to where the money and jewels are buried.

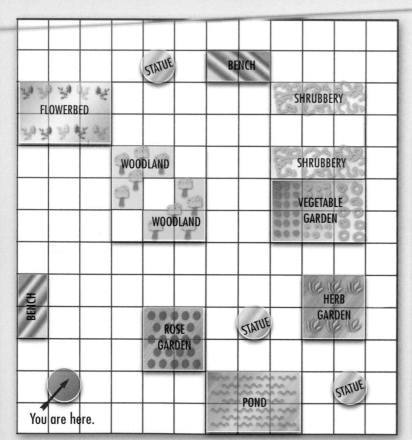

Use the map of the gardens (*left*) to help you follow the directions written in the note (*below*).

Where in the garden are the stolen goods buried?

WHERE TO DIG

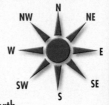

- 3 squares north
- 6 squares east
- 2 squares southeast (diagonally)
- 2 squares east
- 7 squares north
- 6 squares west
- 1 square south
- 2 squares southwest (diagonally)
- 2 squares west
- 3 squares north (DIG HERE!)

Forensics Fact

All living things are made up of cells. Inside most cells, stored as a substance called DNA, are the instructions for making that particular person, animal, or plant. By testing blood, saliva, skin, and hair (if there is some hair root present), forensic scientists can match the DNA found at a crime scene to a suspect. A forensic scientist could find DNA in a single skin cell, which means that just by touching something, such as a doorknob, a person is probably leaving behind his or her DNA. The DNA from the blood and hair found at the millionaire's mansion could be tested to match it to the gardener.

Math Challenge

You found the stolen money and jewels buried exactly where the note directed you. Now you can return them to the millionaire.

If you cut some of the jewels in half, they would look like the shapes pictured below. If you held the cut edge of each jewel against a mirror, what shape would be reflected in the mirror?

1)

2)

3)

4)

MATH TIPS

Detective Work

Multiplication is the same as doing repeated addition.
Example: 5×3 is the same as $5 + 5 + 5$.

Math Challenge

The 12 times table is:

$12 \times 1 = 12$
$12 \times 2 = 24$
$12 \times 3 = 36$
$12 \times 4 = 48$
$12 \times 5 = 60$
$12 \times 6 = 72$
$12 \times 7 = 84$
$12 \times 8 = 96$
$12 \times 9 = 108$
$12 \times 10 = 120$
$12 \times 11 = 132$
$12 \times 12 = 144$

An equilateral triangle has three sides that are all the same length and three angles that are all the same size.

An isosceles triangle has two sides that are the same length and two angles that are the same size.

Evidence Work

TOP TIP: Look carefully at the walls of the room. Notice where the doorway, French doors, and items of furniture are located.

Math Challenge

To find coordinates on a grid map, count the squares along the bottom first, then count upward.

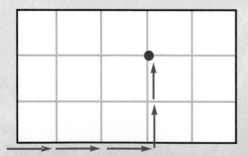

Example: For a grid reference of (3,2), count 3 squares along the bottom, then 2 squares up, to find the exact spot.

Detective Work

TOP TIP: If it takes 1 minute to run 200 yards, then it will take twice as long (2 minutes) to run 400 yards.

Evidence Work

TOP TIP: To find all the details that are different, it will help to examine and compare the photographs, section by section.

Math Challenge

An estimate is not a guess. It is an answer that we know will be close to what is exactly correct. Being good at estimating can help you check your math.

Detective Work

The following tips will help you with your detecting:
- The delivery man does not own white athletic shoes and is shorter than the height of the garden wall.
- The jogger never wears glasses.
- The maid is shorter than the height of the garden wall.

28

PAGES 18–19

Forensic Work

The bars on a bar graph should always be the same width. It is the heights of the bars that are used to compare things. To work with a bar graph, you need to know what each bar stands for. You also need to know the graph's unit of measurement and its scale, such as whether measurements go up by 1s, 2s, 5s, 10s, 100s, 1,000s, or some other amount.

PAGES 20–21

Math Challenge

A tally is made by drawing four vertical lines (IIII), then drawing another line diagonally across the four lines for a total of five lines. You can use your knowledge of the 5 times (multiplication) table to quickly add tally marks.

PAGES 24–25

Math Challenge

You can create a secret code by giving each letter of the alphabet a number. To make the code hard to crack, make the number 1 stand for the first letter of your name, instead of the letter "A," then continue numbering from that letter. If, for example, your name is George or Grace, your code grid would look like this:

1	2	3	4	5	6	7
G	H	I	J	K	L	M
8	9	10	11	12	13	14
N	O	P	Q	R	S	T
15	16	17	18	19	20	21
U	V	W	X	Y	Z	A
22	23	24	25	26		
B	C	D	E	F		

PAGES 26–27

Detective Work

TOP TIP: Use the compass rose pictured on the note for help with directions. Remember that, no matter which way you face, north is always in the same direction.

A "diagonal" is a line that crosses a square from one corner to the opposite corner.

ANSWERS

PAGES 6–7

Detective Work

1) $5,500 was stolen.
2) The **equilateral triangle** is in the ruby box.
   The **square** is in the sapphire box.
   The **octagon** is in the diamond box.
   The **isoceles triangle** is in the sapphire box.
   The **hexagon** is in the ruby box.
3) a) value of all sapphires stolen: $5,950
   b) value of all rubies stolen: $5,850
   c) value of all diamonds stolen: $8,000

Math Challenge

The combination to the safe is: **24 12 36 72 48**

PAGES 8–9

Evidence Work

Sketch B is the correct "picture" of the dining room because the doorway, French doors, and furniture are in the same positions as in the photograph on page 8.

Math Challenge

1) a) splashes of blood on broken glass b) a single hair and a fingerprint c) muddy footprints
2) Fingerprints were found on the table, on the fireplace, and in the safe.
3) A palm print was found on the table.

PAGES 10–11

Detective Work

1) a) 5 minutes b) 7 ½ minutes c) 7 minutes
2) a) 5 minutes 3) 1½ minutes longer

Math Challenge

The following routes visit each location on the mansion grounds once, starting and ending at the main gate.

8, 3, 1, 4, 7	6, 1, 2, 5, 8
7, 5, 3, 1, 6	7, 4, 1, 3, 8

PAGES 12–13

Evidence Work

1) You should have found 10 differences.
2) The following details make dining room B different from dining room A:
- There is a painting next to the cabinet.
- There is a painting over the fireplace.
- The light switch by the doorway is missing.
- The dining room rug is smaller.
- A carving at the top of the cabinet is missing.
- The painting hiding the safe is straight.
- There are normal windows instead of French doors.
- The chandelier above the table is missing.
- There is a dog in the room.
- The flowers on the table are missing.

Math Challenge

There are 26 fingerprints on pages 12 and 13.

PAGES 14–15

Detective Work

1) One person, the jogger, never wears glasses.
2) The delivery man does not own white athletic shoes.
3) The secretary and the chauffeur are the same height.
4) The jogger (6' 6") is the tallest. The maid (59") is the shortest. The difference is 19 inches.
5) The suspects are the secretary, the gardener, the chef, the butler, the personal trainer, the chauffeur, and the handyman.

Math Challenge

With eyes A, you could make 9 different faces.

EYES	MOUTH	NOSE
A	A	A
	A	B
	A	C
	B	A
	B	B
	B	C
	C	A
	C	B
	C	C

You could make the same number of faces with eyes B or C, so the total number possible is 27 different faces.

PAGES 16–17

Detective Work

The following suspects could have been at the mansion between 3:40 p.m. and 4:00 p.m. and had time to commit the crime:

- personal trainer (finished his yoga and weight lifting at 3:30 p.m.)
- chef (finished baking at 3:10 p.m.)
- gardener (finished the rose cuttings at 3:36 p.m.)
- butler (finished writing the work schedule at 3:17 p.m.)
- chauffeur (thinks she returned from the village at about 3:30 p.m.)

The following suspects could not have committed the crime:

- secretary (the handyman saw her leave for the village at 3:30 p.m.)
- handyman (was painting railings until 4:20 p.m.)

Math Challenge

The clock shows 3:40 p.m.

PAGES 18–19

Forensic Work

1) The 12-inch print is shoe size 10. The 11-inch print is shoe size 9.   2) butler, personal trainer, chef, gardener

Math Challenge

1) a) $^{12}/_{36}$ or $^{1}/_{3}$ b) $^{27}/_{36}$ or $^{3}/_{4}$ c) $^{5}/_{60}$ or $^{1}/_{12}$ d) $^{18}/_{60}$ or $^{3}/_{10}$

2) b) $^{3}/_{4}$ = 0.75 d) $^{3}/_{10}$ = 0.3

PAGES 20–21

Forensic Work

BLOOD TYPE	HAIR COLOR	
	brown	not brown
blood type B	🧑🧑	
not blood type B	🧑	🧑

Math Challenge

1) a total of 36 customers 2) 28 customers did not have white hair 3) $^{1}/_{6}$ of the total customers have dyed hair

PAGES 22–23

Forensic Work

1) gardener   2) gardener   3) millionaire
4) gardener   5) millionaire

Math Challenge

1) The palm print belongs to the gardener.
To answer questions 2 and 3, measure the length and width of your palm in inches and calculate the area.
1 square inch = 6.4516 square centimeters.

PAGES 24–25

Detective Work

The message reads: GO TO THE TREE SOUTH OF THE GREENHOUSE AND NORTHWEST OF THE TENNIS COURT AND LOOK IN THE HOLE IN THE TRUNK.

PAGES 26–27

Detective Work

The stolen goods are buried in the flowerbed.

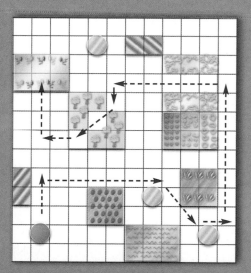

Math Challenge

1) hexagon   2) octagon   3) rectangle   4) triangle

GLOSSARY

ACCOMPLICE a person who assists in activity that is wrong or illegal

ARREST to restrain or take into custody under the authority of the law

ARSON the intentional destruction of property, such as a building, by setting fire to it

CONTAMINATING mixing one item or substance with another, making either or both inferior or impure

CONVICT (v) to find a suspect guilty of a crime or wrongdoing

DECIPHER figure out the meaning of something that is vague or unclear or has been put into some kind of code

DNA short for deoxyribonucleic acid, which is a substance found in the cells of living things and contains the instructions that define how individual people, animals, or plants are made

ENHANCEMENT the process of adding to or improving the value or quality of an object or information

EVIDENCE items and clues, such as hairs, cloth fibers, blood, fingerprints, and footprints, found at a crime scene, which may help prove when, how, and by whom the crime was committed

EVIDENCE TECHNICIAN a person who is specially trained to identify, gather, and safeguard evidence related to a crime

FORENSIC having to do with the use of scientific knowledge to discover facts related to a crime or some other problem that might be debated in a court of law

LATENT present, but often inactive, and cannot be seen with the naked eye without the use of special lights or chemicals

PATENT visible and able to be inspected

PERPETRATOR a person who perpetrates, or commits, a crime

PROSECUTION the process of taking formal legal action in a court of law against someone accused of commiting a crime or violating the law in some other way

RECOVERED gathered and correctly packaged pieces of evidence found at a crime scene

STATEMENTS verbal or written reports or accounts of events and observations taken from victims, witnesses, or suspects by police officers and other official crime investigators to add to or support other evidence related to a crime

SUSPECTS the individuals who law enforcement officials believe, based on evidence and other circumstances, could have committed a particular crime

THREE-DIMENSIONAL not flat, or two-dimensional, having depth as well as length and width

VICINITY a surrounding area that is relatively close by

VICTIMS the people directly affected or harmed by criminals or wrongdoers

WITNESSES people who have seen something happen and are able to provide firsthand information about the occurrence

Measurement Conversions

1 inch = 2.54 centimeters (cm)
1 square inch = 6.4516 square centimeters (sq cm)
1 yard = 0.9144 meters (m)